THIS WALKER BOOK BELONGS TO:

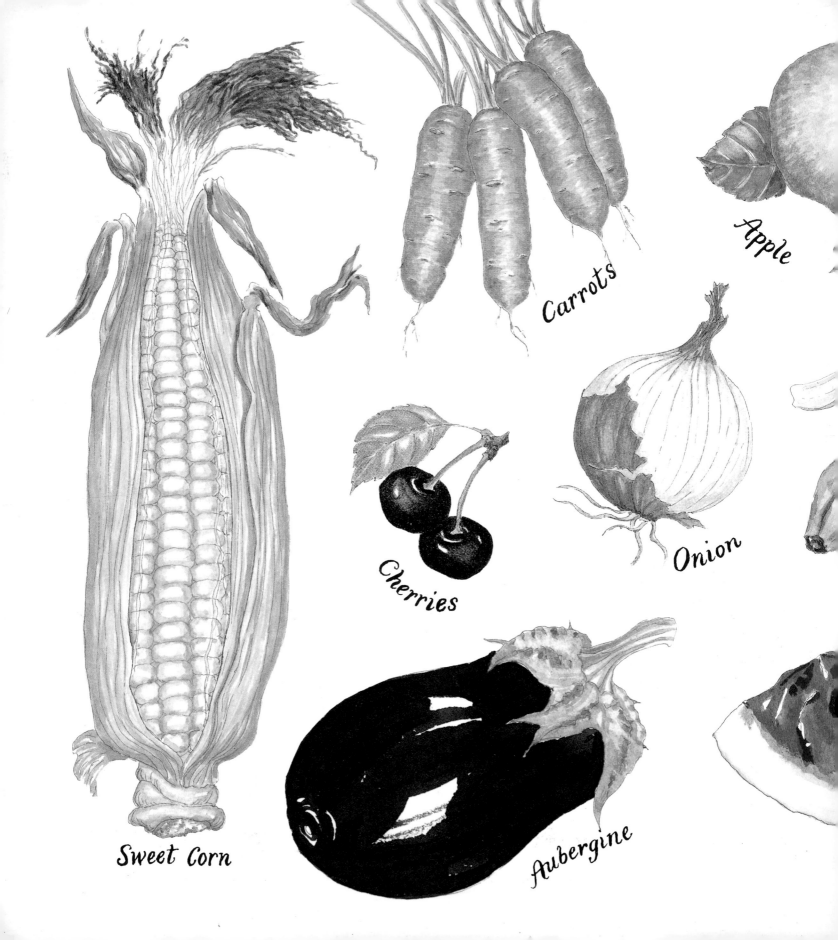

Carrots

Apple

Cherries

Onion

Sweet Corn

Aubergine

Potato

Banana

H ave you ever been to the market to buy fruit and vegetables? Did you ever wonder where they came from, and how they grew before you took them home to your kitchen? You may have seen an apple tree heavy with apples, but have you ever seen a banana tree? Or a sprouting potato?

Each fruit and vegetable begins as part of a growing plant with roots, stems, leaves, flowers and seeds. And each one – juicy, crunchy, crisp or squashy – has its own special character.

I hope all the fruits and vegetables that appear in this book will give you as much pleasure as they give me.

Scarlet Runner Beans

Watermelon

Strawberry

Orange

To my daughter Anna

P.K.

First published 1993 by
Walker Books Ltd
87 Vauxhall Walk
London SE11 5HJ

This edition published 1996

2 4 6 8 10 9 7 5 3 1

© 1993 Phyllis King

This book has been typeset
in ITC Garamond light.

Printed in Hong Kong

British Library Cataloguing in Publication Data
A catalogue record for this book is
available from the British Library.

ISBN 0-7445-4733-4

Apple Green
and Runner Bean

Written and illustrated by

Phyllis King

WALKER BOOKS
AND SUBSIDIARIES
LONDON • BOSTON • SYDNEY

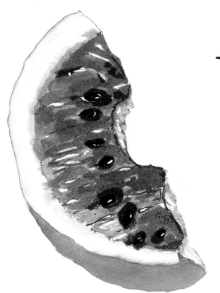

Watermelon

What could be nicer
on a hot, thirsty day
than a juicy
watermelon ?

The heavy green
fruit breaks open
with a great cracking
sound, and there
inside lie the shiny
black pips, embedded
in glistening pink flesh.
Eating watermelon is more
like having a drink, with the juice
running down your chin and making
little rivers down your arms.

Watermelon seeds—the pips—can be dried and eaten.

If you eat it outside, then
nobody minds the drips
and you spit out the pips
as far as you can.

In hot countries, like Spain,
you can see watermelons
growing round and heavy
in the sun, attached to
their trailing vine.

tendril

melon flower

prickly vine

7

Sweet Corn

If you had a garden
you could grow
sweet corn and
pick your cobs off
the tall stalks.
You would have to
stretch up to
pick them, because
the plant grows
taller than your mum
and the cobs lie right
up against the stalk.

tassels

husks

Sweet corn is one kind of maize.
Popcorn is another.

The flowers become
the tassels on
an ear of corn.

If you don't grow
corn, you can buy it
at the market. You
can peel off the husks
and silken tassels that
cover the cob and see
the yellow kernels
lying in rows like
teeth. Then you can
boil the cob and
sink *your* teeth
into it.

An ear of corn looks like
this. The core of it is the cob.

Cherry

The cherry tree in spring, covered in pure white blossom, is a wonderful sight.

But just as wonderful is the cherry tree in summer, its branches bending with juicy red cherries waiting to be picked.

After the petals fall, the cherries begin to grow.

Cherries can be black or red.

When I was a child, my uncle had a cherry tree in his garden. He would let us come to pick and eat as many cherries as we could reach.

By the time we had finished picking and eating, our fingers and mouths were stained dark red with juice, and our tummies were full.

Scarlet Runner Bean

The scarlet runner
bean is a magical plant.
The stems, twisting
and winding up the
tall pole, remind me
of Jack's beanstalk.
The brilliant scarlet
flowers are like drops
of blood. Long green
pods hang in clusters
among the leaves.

A bean pod can be over 50 centimetres long.

But the most exciting thing about the runner bean is opening the pod. There, quietly glowing, are the beans, looking as though they've been painted with a fine brush. Pink, and mottled with dark purple, they lie resplendent in their green bed.

As each flower dies, a bean pod begins to form.

A bean is a seed!

13

strawberry flower

Strawberry

Squatting down
in a strawberry field
is the way I like to eat
strawberries.
Some people like
them in a dish with
cream and sugar, but
I like them best warm
and sweet with the
sun, straight from
the plant.

At a strawberry farm
you can pick your own,
down on your knees.
The best ones are
often hidden under the
leaves. While you fill
your basket, you can
fill your mouth too.
And when you get home,
you can help make
strawberry jam.

Potato

Potatoes don't lie on the ground, ripening in the sun. They like to be in the cool dark ground with earth humped up on top of them.

When you plant a potato in the earth, some of its shoots grow upwards to become stems and leaves.

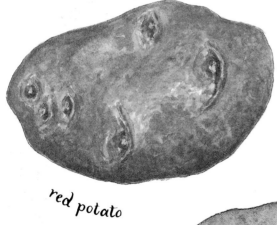

red potato

Shoots grow from the "eyes" of a potato.

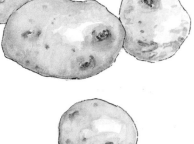

potato flower

potato chips

And some of its
shoots grow downwards,
swelling at the ends to form
tiny new potatoes. When the
potatoes have grown to their
full size, the plant above
the ground begins to die.
Then it is time to dig up
these cool beauties
from their earthy nest.

early potatoes

Apple

If you've got an
apple tree in your back
garden, you'll have
seen the branches
loaded with apples.
You may have watched
them growing.
In spring the boughs
are lovely, with delicate
pink blossoms.

When the petals have
fallen, tiny green apples
begin to form.

All summer they are growing bigger, but still your mum won't let you pick one. "Wait till they're ripe," she says. And it's worth waiting, because unripe apples are hard and taste sour… But bite into a ripe apple! Its juice and fresh sweetness will burst into your mouth.

Cut an apple in half, sideways, and you'll see a star, made of the seeds in their beds.

Ripe apples can be green, red, yellow or rosy pink.

Onion

What I like best about an onion is peeling off the thin, stiff outer skins. They tear with a crackly sound, like tissue paper. In fact the skin is rather like tissue paper. Hold a piece up to the light and see how the light glows through it. You can almost see through it. You can write your name on it.

An onion is a bulb, made up of swollen leaf-bases.

20

Chives belong to the same plant family as onions...

Once you've peeled away its paper-like skin, you'll find wet, whitish layers of onion flesh. And here lies the onion's secret. As the knife cuts into its firm shape, your eyes will begin to water. A cut onion can make you cry!

You eat the leaves of chives.

Let a grown-up do the chopping!

Banana

Bananas only grow in hot climates.

You can use a banana leaf as a plate or an umbrella.

Unzip a banana!
No, bananas don't really
have zips, but as you peel
open their yellow jackets
it seems as though they should.

If you've ever lived in the
Caribbean, Bangladesh
or parts of Africa, you'll have
seen bananas growing on
tall plants with huge
flapping leaves.

One mighty
stem bends with the
weight of hundreds
of bananas
spiralling
round it.

banana flower

The stem is
cut down while the
bananas are still green, but
by the time you get them, they
are yellow and ready to eat.
So, unzip a banana!

23

The carrot you eat is the root of the plant.

Carrot

I never liked cooked carrots when I was a child, but I ate lots of raw ones from my dad's vegetable garden.

If you leave a carrot in the ground, it will make a flower next year.

carrot flower

After I'd helped to pull out weeds, he'd let me pull up a carrot. I'd wash it under the tap and eat it, holding the stems with their beautiful lacy leaves.

Some people say that carrots make your eyes bright. Other people say they make your hair curl, but I don't think that's true, because my hair is not a bit curly.

Orange

An orange grove is like an enchanted orchard: row upon row of small glossy trees, with balls of golden fruit hanging among the shining foliage.

Navel oranges have no seeds.

Open an orange, and as
you start to peel the skin
the pungent aroma of
orange oil spurts and oozes
from its pores. Your hands
will be wet with oil before
you've even got to the
juicy orange. And when
you've finished sucking
and eating, the memory
lingers on your fingers.

Seville oranges
are good for making
marmalade.

Orange peel
is full of oil
glands.

The whitish
part is called
the "pith."

Orange
Marmalade

Another name for the aubergine is "egg plant".

Aubergine

How strange and beautiful is the aubergine. Its firm globe shape is glossy purple-black and satin smooth. When you hold it, you can't imagine what the inside will be like. It feels both heavy and light. There is no smell. Will it be juicy? Will the flesh be purple?

The aubergine is a fruit, but it is eaten as a vegetable.

Cut it open.
Now you get the smell –
faint and slightly bitter.
And what a surprise!
No juice, but spongy,
cream-coloured flesh
with a pattern of tiny
soft seeds.

How will you eat
this exotic creature?
Will you slice it in
thick rounds to fry,
or put it in a curry?

Aubergines can be purple or white.

Potato

Scarlet
Runner Beans

Banana

Index

Look up the pages to find out about
all these fruits and vegetables.
Don't forget to look at both
kinds of words:
this kind and *this kind*.

Orange

Strawberry

Watermelon

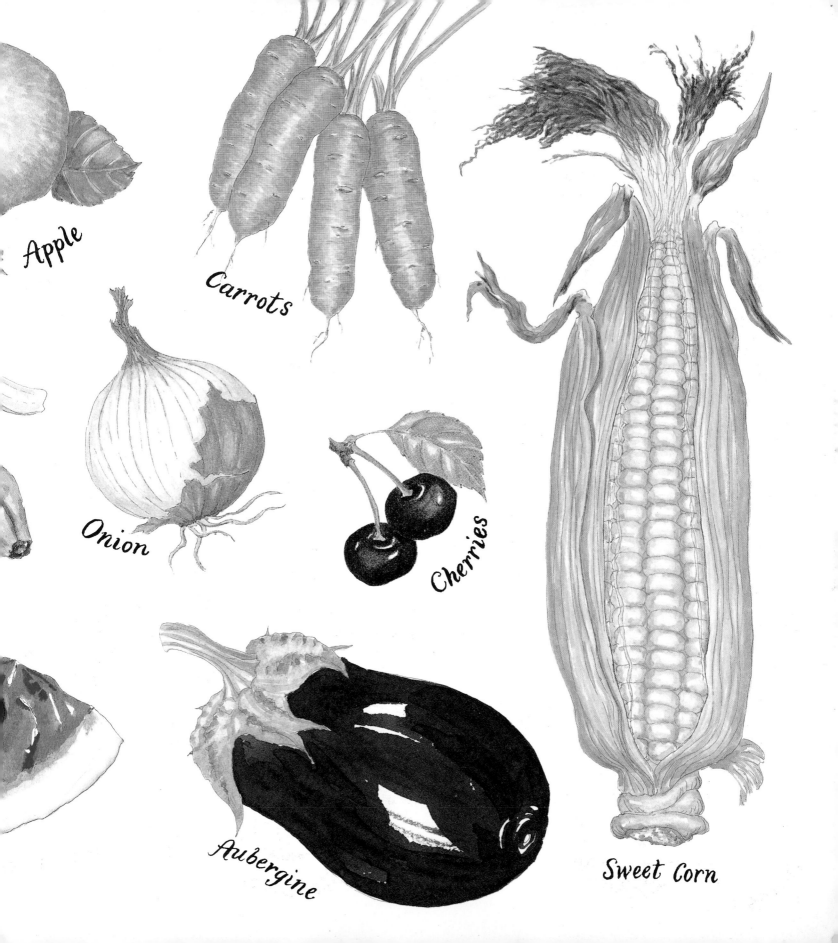

Apple

Carrots

Onion

Cherries

Aubergine

Sweet Corn

MORE WALKER PAPERBACKS
For You to Enjoy

An award-winning series of non-fiction picture books
full of facts and feelings about the real world.

"These books fulfil all the requirements of a factual picture book,
but also supply that imaginative element." *The Independent on Sunday*

"Beautifully illustrated books, written with style and humour."
The Times Educational Supplement

RED FOX by Karen Wallace/Peter Melnyczuk   0-7445-4361-4

I LOVE GUINEA-PIGS by Dick-King Smith/Anita Jeram   0-7445-4725-3

ALL PIGS ARE BEAUTIFUL by Dick-King Smith/Anita Jeram   0-7445-3635-9

THE APPLE TREES by Vivian French/Terry Milne   0-7445-4731-8

TOWN PARROT by Penelope Bennett/Sue Heap   0-7445-4727-X

THINK OF AN EEL by Karen Wallace/Mike Bostock   0-7445-3639-1
(Winner of the Times Educational Supplement Junior Information
Book Award and the Kurt Maschler Award)

CATERPILLAR CATERPILLAR by Vivian French/Charlotte Voake   0-7445-3636-7

I LIKE MONKEYS BECAUSE… by Peter Hansard/Patricia Casey   0-7445-3646-4

A FIELD FULL OF HORSES by Peter Hansard/Kenneth Lilly   0-7445-3645-6

THIS BOWL OF EARTH by Jan Mark/Gay Shephard   0-7445-4729-6

THE MUSHROOM HUNT by Simon Frazer/Penny Dale   0-7445-4732-6

£4.99 each